Zodiac Signs

LEO

DiscoverRoo
An Imprint of Pop!
popbooksonline.com

by Elizabeth Andrews

WELCOME TO DiscoverRoo!

This book is filled with videos, puzzles, games, and more! Scan the QR codes* while you read, or visit the website below to make this book pop.

popbooksonline.com/leo

abdobooks.com
Published by Pop!, a division of ABDO, PO Box 398166, Minneapolis, Minnesota 55439.

Printed in the United States of America, North Mankato, Minnesota.
042025
082025

THIS BOOK CONTAINS RECYCLED MATERIALS

Cover Photo: Splendoura Prints; Shutterstock Images
Interior Photos: Alamy Stock Photo; Getty Images; Shutterstock Images
Editor: Tyler Gieseke
Series Designer: Laura Graphenteen

Library of Congress Control Number: 2024948385

Publisher's Cataloging-in-Publication Data
Names: Andrews, Elizabeth, author.
Title: Leo / by Elizabeth Andrews
Description: Minneapolis, Minnesota : Pop!, 2026 | Series: Zodiac signs | Includes online resources and index
Identifiers: ISBN 9781098247911 (lib. bdg.) | ISBN 9781098248451 (ebook)
Subjects: LCSH: Leo (Astrology)--Juvenile literature. | Lion (Astrology)--Juvenile literature. | Zodiac--Juvenile literature. | Astrology--Juvenile literature. | Astrology--Charts, diagrams, etc.--Juvenile literature.
Classification: DDC 133.52--dc23

*Scanning QR codes requires a web-enabled smart device with a QR code reader app and a camera.

TABLE OF CONTENTS

CHAPTER 1

MEET THE LEO!

Leo is the fifth sign of the zodiac. People born between July 23 and August 22 are Leos. When people ask for your "star sign," they are likely asking for your sun sign. This is the zodiac sign the sun appeared in at your birth.

WATCH A VIDEO HERE!

Sunflower

July 23–August 22

LEO

ZODIAC CALENDAR

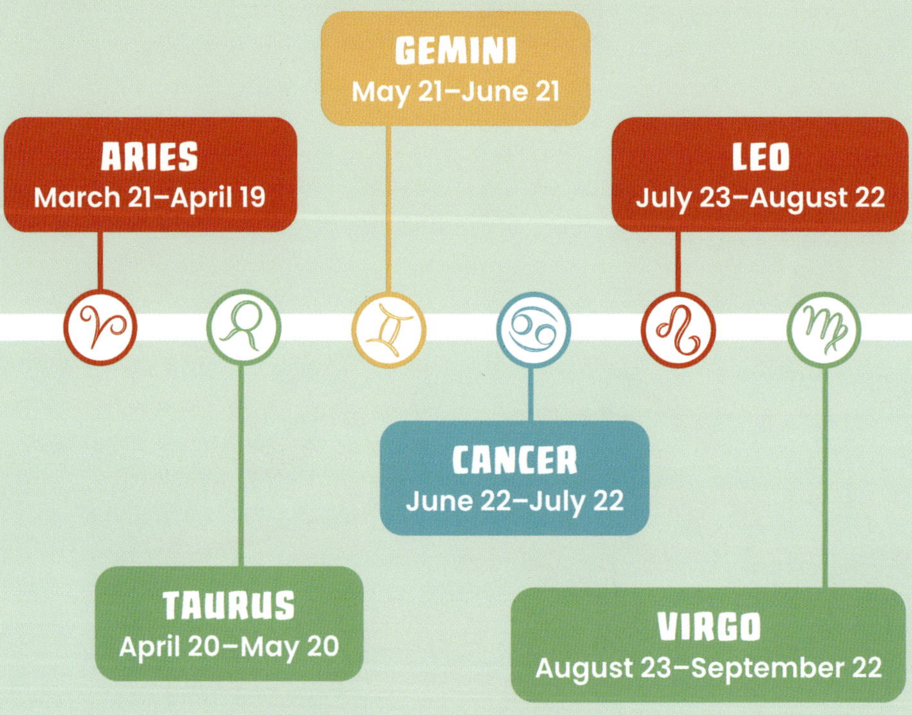

Three features help describe zodiac signs. Signs can be masculine or feminine. Each zodiac sign is given a mode. The three modes are cardinal, fixed, and mutable. Each zodiac is also

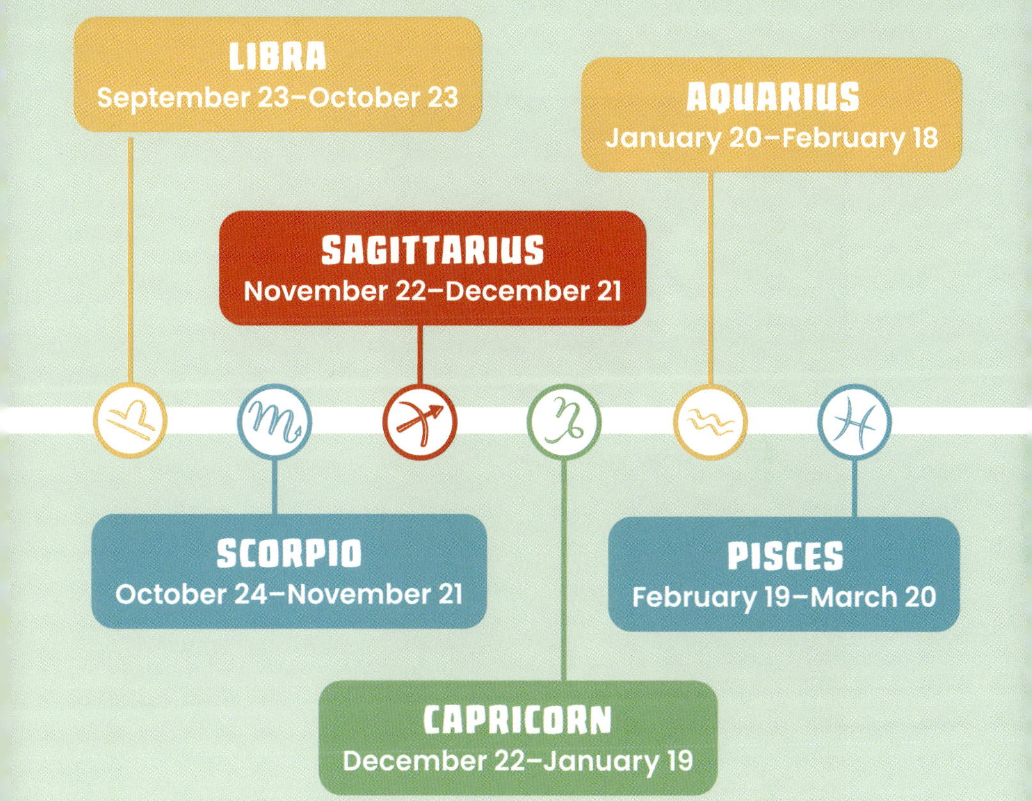

a fire, air, earth, or water sign. No zodiac signs share the same three features.

DID YOU KNOW? Fixed signs are born in the middle of seasons. Depending on where they live, Leos are born in the summer or winter.

Being a masculine sign does not mean Leo is a boyish sign. It is just a way to describe how Leos act.

Leo is a masculine, fixed, fire sign. People with masculine signs are reasonable and action focused. They usually say exactly what they mean. They are outgoing and strong.

Modes describe how signs interact with the outside world. Fixed signs are very grounded. This means that they are emotionally stable and clear thinkers. They don't like change. Leos are active and exciting like most fire signs. They are often bold and dramatic.

Leo is one of the easiest constellations to find in the night sky.

Leos are brave! They enjoy being in the spotlight.

Leo is **represented** by a lion. Lions are royal, brave, proud, and sometimes lazy. Early **astrologers** in Mesopotamia connected the Leo **constellation** to a monster killed by their great hero Gilgamesh. Greeks thought Leo represented the lion killed by Hercules.

DID YOU KNOW?

The lion Hercules killed had golden fur that protected it from weapons.

CHAPTER 2

HISTORY OF ASTROLOGY

Humans have searched for life's **spiritual** meaning since the beginning of time. They often looked to the stars for this. Astrology is the practice of reading the movements of planets and other **celestial** bodies and connecting them to life on Earth.

LEARN MORE HERE!

Some ancient people used the zodiac signs to predict future events.

Babylonians invented the zodiac in Mesopotamia over 5,000 years ago. Mesopotamia was the first known civilization. Babylon was one of the region's largest cities.

Ptolemy was an Egyptian man who studied the stars.

Earth and our solar system are in the Milky Way galaxy.

The zodiac is a belt of space around Earth that has 12 well-known **constellations**. Ancient people noticed that the sun seemed to move in front of these constellations throughout a year. The sun spends about a month in each constellation.

The constellations in the zodiac belt are Aries, Taurus, Gemini, Cancer, Leo, Virgo, Libra, Scorpius, Sagittarius, Capricornus, Aquarius, and Pisces. Together they make up the 12 zodiac signs. They are all **represented** by different **symbols**.

Islamic astrologers created new ways to map and measure stars.

THE ZODIAC WHEEL

DID YOU KNOW?

Most zodiac symbols are animals. The ancient Greeks called the belt of space *zodiakos kyklos,* or "circle of animals."

CHAPTER 3

THE PERFORMER

Leos are ruled by the sun. They are warm, confident, and **charming**. Some people say Leos are like the sun itself because they shine so brightly. Leos were born to do really big things in really big ways.

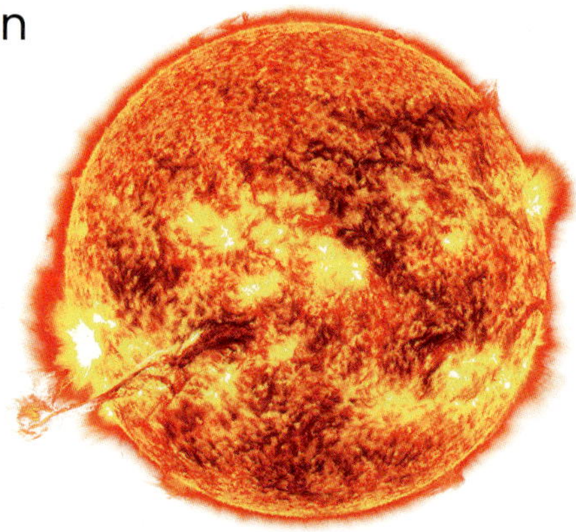

EXPLORE LINKS HERE!

Pop singer Dua Lipa is a Leo. She shines onstage!

Leos' **enthusiasm** feeds into all parts of their life. They are on a journey to find out what they can get out of life. Leos are creatives at heart. They dislike anything dull or ordinary, so they often make their own excitement.

It is important that Leos take time to care for themselves.

Leos are devoted to finding their role in life. They see anything they do as part of themselves. This can be seen in Leos' longing for the finer things in life. Nothing is too good for Leos. If they want something, they go and get it. Leos are the biggest spenders of the zodiac signs.

Kylie Jenner is a Leo. She often wears expensive clothes. Once, she showed off her zodiac sign at a fashion event.

Leos' daily life is a performance. They love attention and respect. Leos care about what people think of them. They want to be adored by all and prefer the adoration be obvious. Leos need to feel needed. However, they would never tell someone that.

Leos' emotions are always larger than life. Anger, love, joy, and sadness are all felt strongly. These big

DID YOU KNOW? Leos are very creative! Working on creative projects makes them happy. They might have a hard time finishing though.

Tom Holland's Spider-Man is a Leo! He is very brave and quick to solve problems.

feelings push Leos to act quickly. Leos approach problems with bravery, and they always believe that they will be successful.

CHAPTER 4

LEOS' KINGDOM

Just as the lions that **represent** them, Leos possess a kingdom. Their kingdom could be their home, family, romantic partner, job, or creative purpose. Leos are willing to do anything for their kingdoms.

COMPLETE AN ACTIVITY HERE!

Martha Stewart is a Leo. She has a large business that represents her kingdom. Martha has followed many of her big dreams.

Leo is a fixed sign. Fixed signs are born in the middle of seasons. It makes them trustworthy.

Leos make great friends. They are very loyal and often give good advice. People love the warmth and **enthusiasm** a Leo can bring into their lives. Their ability to dream big can encourage others to do so as well. Leos get along best with Libras. They are both kind and filled with **passion**.

When it comes to business and work, Leos like to be in charge. They believe they were born to be in powerful positions. It's not something they have to earn. Leos think they always know best. Most people are happy to let Leos take the lead because they are brave when it comes to solving problems. Leos are also very easy to get along with in the workplace.

DID YOU KNOW?

Leos are generous with their time and energy.

Sometimes, when Leos are focused on themselves and their own successes, their egos can become too big. While Leos are bringing joy to the world around them, they may appear as show-offs to other people. But their love of life is what shines through the most!

Fixed signs are usually confident. Leos love being themselves!

Today, astrology can answer questions about an individual. People use astrology to understand who they are and why they might do what they do. It can also help people understand others in their life. A zodiac sign can point out personal skills, possibilities, and **internal motivations**.

WHAT IS A BIRTH CHART?

Each person's birth chart contains all the planets in our solar system, the moon, and the sun. The location of where each **celestial** body was based on the exact time and location of a person's birth can be marked on a birth chart. A birth chart can explain even more about a person than what only a sun sign can. The placement of each planet affects the drive of a person. This reveals personal motivations. Astrology experts can read birth charts.

MAKING CONNECTIONS

TEXT-TO-SELF

Are you a Leo? If so, do you think the sign matches your personality? If not, what do you have in common with Leos?

TEXT-TO-TEXT

Have you read any books about the other zodiac signs? How were those signs similar to and different from Leos?

TEXT-TO-WORLD

With the help of an adult, look up famous Leos. Pick one person and write a few sentences about ways that person shows Leo qualities.

GLOSSARY

astrologers — people who study and practice astrology.

celestial — having to do with the sky or outer space.

charming — very pleasing and delightful.

constellation — a group of stars that forms a pattern.

enthusiasm — strong excitement of feeling.

internal — of, relating to, or being on the inside.

motivation — something that makes one want to do something.

passion — any strong feeling or emotion.

represent — to stand for or be a sign of.

spiritual — having to do with people's beliefs in things such as the soul, nature, and what happens after death.

symbol — an object or picture that represents something else.

INDEX